Tennis Fashions

Over 125 years of Costume Change

Whilst caught up in the excitement of a hard hitting tennis match on Centre Court, in which the world's top class players compete for the honours, aided by the very best clothing and equipment that modern technology can provide, it is perhaps hard to believe that modern Tennis is a direct descendant of a much older game, medieval in origin, known today as Real or Royal Tennis.

King Henry VIII played this ancient game of Tennis with some enthusiasm in his youth. Contemporary sixteenth century accounts indicate that his tennis clothes included a coat rather like a short jacket or jerkin, made in blue and black velvet, probably worn for extra warmth over his doublet on the way to and from the tennis court, "a shirt of the finest texture" through which the King's fair skin positively glowed during the exertion of play, the usual long stockings of the period and shoes with felt soles.

Tennis costume has come a long way since these early accounts of 1519! The story of how these changes have occurred is a fascinating one, and provides considerable insight into the etiquette associated with late 19th- and early 20th-century English social history. The following records some of the milestones along the way.

Throughout its long and regal history, Real Tennis was largely restricted to Royalty and the very wealthy. Ladies, with one or two notable exceptions, simply did not participate. However, when in 1874 Major Walter Wingfield launched his new and improved court for playing his version of Real Tennis out of doors on the lawns of Victorian England, things changed rapidly. Lawn Tennis became all the rage among the upper middle classes, who had the leisure time and the means to participate in sports, and right from the beginning ladies took to the new pastime eagerly.

The rackets and balls associated with Lawn Tennis were lighter than those used in Real Tennis and therefore the new game was more suited to the feminine physique of the time. Mothers with daughters of marriageable age, if a little guarded at first, were soon suitably delighted by the new game, which provided ample social opportunity for meeting eligible partners of the opposite sex.

There was however one immediate and overriding problem that had to be overcome by these first lady players and that was the question of what to wear. Every other aspect of a Victorian lady's life was governed by a strict code of etiquette. For the new game there were no precedents. Ladies of good breeding had not previously been included in outdoor pastimes which involved attempting to run about in the heat of the summer sunshine, or incurring the risk of perspiration, soiled shoes and clothing, or worst of all perhaps, acquiring a tanned or freckled skin and thus being associated with the labouring classes who worked out of doors. They were under immense social pressure to appear attractive, tidy and unruffled at all times, and fair skins were protected from the horrors of freckles and tanning by elaborate hats and parasols.

In the face of all this, the first lady players, eager to participate,

A ladies' doubles in progress in 1879. The participants' clothes are pretty but impractical. Tennis aprons were worn to prevent dresses from becoming soiled. They were often made at home and decorated with elaborate embroidery.

Frills and flounces were all the rage for garden party tennis in 1886, when attracting admiring glances was just as important as being proficient at the new Lawn Tennis.

yet loathe to offend, resorted to wearing exactly the type of clothes they would have worn to a garden party. In the 1870s and the 1880s therefore, while the men were comfortably kitted out as for cricket, ladies' tennis clothing made no concession to comfort or commonsense, with far more emphasis placed upon looking pretty at all times and following fashion, however impractical, than upon the requirement of being able to move and breathe easily.

Elaborately flounced, ground length dresses were the order of the day. Sleeves were long and ornamented, necklines were high and waists were clinched. Straw hats were decorated with ribbons and flowers. Underpinnings were equally complicated and consisted of boned corsets, a bustle and layers of petticoats worn over long drawers and stockings. Originally even ladies' lawn tennis shoes had heels, but one of the first concessions was to adopt flat, indiarubber-soled shoes, usually in black, so that any grass stains or scuff marks would go unnoticed.

Most Victorian ladies had their dresses made up by local seamstresses who relied upon the fashion magazines for hints and patterns. *Isobel's Dressmaking* in 1886 advised: "In tennis dresses fancy has taken full play and each lady can design her own".

Coloured serge, flannel and cotton were popular fabrics of the time. Stripes, decorative trims and embroidered panels were also favoured. "Norfolk" jackets were considered sporty and appropriate, worn over contrasting skirts, and costumes were frequently made up in a combination of different fabrics.

Tennis aprons were useful accessories. They protected dresses from becoming soiled, and often had large pockets for holding tennis balls. This avoided as much as possible the difficult task of bending to pick up tennis balls. The *Field* in 1885 makes mention of: "A costume of pale blue flannel with deep kilted skirt and long basque bodice, an embroidered apron with pocket to hold the balls and a long overcoat which is intended for playing".

Unsuitable garments

However, even as early as the 1880s, in spite of all the social pressure to conform, there was a growing realisation of the unsuitability of these garden party clothes for lady players. Cartoons appeared in *Punch* throughout the 1870s and 1880s, depicting ladies trying to play Lawn Tennis in ridiculously unsuitable garments.

Other contemporary publications such as *Pastime* and the *Field* printed letters from inflamed correspondents, either lauding or opposing the merits of dress reform for lady players. In 1885 the *Field* noted that: "The present healthy custom of indulging in active outdoor amusements is sadly interfered with by the ordinary costume ... Lawn Tennis has taught women how much they are capable of doing and it is a sign of the times that various games and sports which have been tabooed a few years ago as "unladylike" are actually encouraged at various girls schools!!" *Pastime* in 1886, pinpoints one of the chief problems with ladies' tennis wear at the time, in that it is described as: "being generally speaking, tight where it should be loose; and loose where it should be tight".

Things must have been desperate for the *Queen* magazine in 1880 to depict two lady players in "rationals" or bloomers! The cry for a bloomer style costume was also taken up by a brave correspondent in *Pastime* in 1886 who, identified only as "A Lawn Tennis Player", proposed that ladies would be better served by adopting a costume along the lines of: "Moorish trousers loose and

Whilst the first lady players were hampered by all the constraints of corsets and long skirts, the men were comparatively comfortably kitted out. H. F. Lawford v. W. Renshaw from the Graphic, 1881.

gathered in at the ankles, made of silk or some other suitable material, a short skirt in the same, I believe only just covering the knees, or an open Moorish bodice".

Victorian society in the 1880s however, was not ready to accept the prospect of its womenfolk adopting this risqué style of costume, which, in the words of another correspondent, "would hardly be indicative of good taste". This was particularly the case in view of the fact that increasingly play took place in public. Even Oscar Wilde is quoted in the *Pall Mall Gazette*, in 1884 as referring to "the ugliness, the want of proportion in the bloomer costume which in other respects is sensible".

Thus it was that the fear of appearing "unladylike" continued to hamper major dress reform for lady players up until the end of the 19th century, with the effects of this attitude lasting well into the first part of the 20th century.

However, one problem which simply had to be addressed very early on was that of perspiration. As increased skill at the game led to more movement on Court, this in turn led to the dreaded

Leading lady players at The Irish Championships held at the Fitzwilliam Club, Dublin in 1888, show their preference for all-white copies of contemporary fashionable dress, complemented by the sporty straw boater.

problem of perspiration causing the appearance of embarrassing damp patches on coloured fabrics. It was quite unthinkable that a lady should be seen to perspire!

It was the Irish who as well as being the first to permit a Ladies' Championship, at the Fitzwilliam Club, Dublin in 1879, came up with the clever solution to this delicate problem. All white copies of contemporary fashionable clothes were found to be the answer, and throughout the 1880s all-white tennis clothes became quite the hallmark of the more proficient lady players, and almost a symbol of their dedication to the game itself, rather than to the social scene associated with it.

During the 1880s, a small band of seasoned and highly dedicated lady players were seen competing regularly at tournaments up and down the country, at places such as Edgbaston, Cheltenham, Bath and Exmouth, and of course from 1884 onwards at Wimbledon. It was during these years that the names of pioneering spirits such as Maud Watson, Blanche Bingley (Mrs. Hillyard) and Lottie Dod began to appear on The

Championship rolls of honour at Wimbledon.

Maud Watson won her first Wimbledon Championship in 1884 wearing an all-white two-piece costume with a bustle and elaborate draperies around the hips. Her skirt was ankle-length and was worn with black shoes and stockings. She preferred the sporty and more business-like look of the man's straw boater to that of the fussy and feminine hats worn by the less good players. The second lady Champion, Blanche Bingley (1886) wore a very similar costume to that of Maud Watson, except that for some unknown reason, she was in the habit of also wearing white kid gloves.

Lottie Dod, who won the Ladies' Singles at Wimbledon five times in all, had something of an advantage over her opponents when she first won in 1887, because being only 15 years old, it was just acceptable for her to play in a costume almost the same as her school uniform. Her calf-length dress allowed her more freedom of movement. She wore black stockings and shoes and a jaunty white cricket cap completed her attire. Later on in her career, she wore a

Left: Maud Watson who won the first Ladies' Singles Championship at Wimbledon, in 1884. Right: Maud's older sister Lilian was runner-up in the same final.

Above, Lottie Dod in her just acceptable calf-length skirt, 1887 and May Sutton with her sleeves rolled up, 1905. Below, Muriel Robb and Charlotte Sterry - two examples of Edwardian elegance on court.

loose terracotta long sleeved blouse with close-fitting embroidered collar and cuffs surmounting a dark blue skirt. She was a true sportswoman, successful in other sports as well as Lawn Tennis, and as such she is quoted in 1905 as appealing for: "A suitable attire for women's tennis which does not impede breathing" and also: "Hearty indeed would be the thanks of puzzled lady players to the individual who invented an easy and pretty costume".

Throughout the 1890s, ladies' tennis costume remained very much an all-white version of everyday summer wear. By the turn of the century, the bustle had completely disappeared and the hat likewise was shortly to follow suit. The fashion was for heavy, full, white skirts, hanging two to three inches off the ground, worn with a crisp cotton, or later on a muslin blouse, over starched petticoats which might be trimmed with "broderie anglaise" frills at the ankles.

Popular material

Cotton piqué was a popular material for skirts. It washed well and hung beautifully. The necklines of blouses were quite severe with stiff and starchy collars and cuffs, worn with men's neck ties and coloured "petersham" belts fastened with decorative buckles, but towards the end of the Edwardian era, this look softened to feature frilled "jabot" or modest "V" necklines.

Those who risked censure in their quest for comfort in the early 1900s include Charlotte Sterry (Mrs. Cooper), who in 1904 raised her hemline by a tentative two inches and May Sutton, from the U.S.A., who caused quite a stir by playing at Wimbledon in 1905 with her sleeves rolled up because she was hot. Some said that for ease of movement she even used to play in her father's shirts! With this costume she wore a headband, tied with a bow, white stockings and white shoes. The silhouette however remained that of the hourglass, achieved only through the agonies of uncomfortable steel-boned corsets and stays. It was to take World War 1, bringing a halt to play and fashion consciousness, together with a change in attitudes, to free lady players once and for all from the tyranny of corsets.

But before moving on to the exciting developments which were to occur in ladies' tennis costume in the twenties, what of the men? We know that they suffered relatively little from the restrictions of fashion, but what exactly did they wear and what were their choices in the years before 1914?

From the beginning gentlemen's tennis wear was casual, combining comfort and ease. In the 1880s and 1890s well cut cream or white flannel trousers and long-sleeved flannel shirts were the norm. Shirts were buttoned to the neck and worn with a short silk tie, which might be spotted or striped, the ends being squared off. Trousers were a generous length over shoes, to allow for shrinkage after many washes. Turn-ups became fashionable during the Edwardian era. Long shirt sleeves might be neatly rolled up to the elbow. Trousers were held up by means of either striped or coloured belts with "S" buckles or sometimes by means of gaily patterned "kerchiefs" or sashes, wrapped and tied around the waist. There are records of lady players complaining about the sight of gentlemen players constantly hitching up their trousers during play when the sash was adopted, so obviously belts were better for the serious player, or even perhaps as advertised in *Pastime* in 1886, "British Argosy Braces" described as being "best for Lawn Tennis".

Quite often caps were worn, these being made in Club or University colours to match the blazers that became increasingly popular. These were single-breasted, usually fastened quite high at the lapel, with three to four buttons. Shoes were made of kid leather, which might be two-tone in colour, or canvas, and had rubber soles. They were sold bearing names such as "The Tenacious" Tennis Shoe, suggesting that they were designed to give a good grip on sometimes slippery grass surfaces. Socks were usually black or brown wool.

Tailored look

In the 1870s and 1880s some players preferred to wear cream knickerbockers, fastened at the knee, in conjunction with thick dark socks, rather than long trousers. Herbert Lawford, a big man, preferred this style which he wore with a striped "Rugby" style shirt. In contrast, one of his chief opponents, William Renshaw, along with his twin brother Ernest, preferred the more tailored look, described above. The *Gentleman's Magazine of Fashion*, in 1882, referred to the fact that with tennis fashion "opinion is equally divided between trousers and knickerbockers".

Above, Herbert Lawford preferred the knickerbocker costume, whereas in the 1880s, the Renshaw twins favoured a more tailored look. By the turn of the century, the Doherty brothers (below) impressed spectators with their immaculate appearance and their brilliant play.

Suzanne Lenglen arrived at Wimbledon in 1919 like a breath of fresh air. Soon the one-piece Lenglen style frock and colourful bandeau were all the rage amongst fashion conscious ladies, both on and off the court.

Through the 1880s and well into the early 1900s, the "Owe Forty" or blanket coat was worn to and from the court. This was like a large long overcoat, made from cream wool blanket material with a pleat at the back and a tie belt. This was thrown over tennis attire with a certain casual elegance, to help both male and female players keep warm – rather like an early version of the track suit of more modern times!

At the turn of the century the Doherty brothers, who between them won Wimbledon many times, impressed the crowds with their brilliant play and with their immaculate appearance. They were very much the gentlemen of the courts and set a new trend by wearing their shirt sleeves long and unbuttoned at the cuffs, in a form of languid elegance. Otherwise, neatly rolled shirt sleeves were the norm until short sleeves appeared in conjunction with shorts in the 1930s.

The First World War changed many things, including attitudes to women in sport. Women themselves, having had to take on much during the war years that would previously have been considered the preserve of men, were in the mood to pursue their own emancipation with more determination. Against this background, it was the dramatic appearance at Wimbledon in 1919 of a daring and brilliant young French woman, Suzanne Lenglen, which was to provide the focal point for the attack upon the restraints of tradition.

New guard

When Suzanne defeated Dorothea Lambert Chambers in the Ladies' Singles Final it was in many ways a victory for the new guard against the old. Dorothea, already seven times a Wimbledon winner, played hampered by an ankle-length gored white skirt, worn over petticoats and a corset, with a plain long-sleeved shirt kept buttoned at her wrists. Suzanne however, arrived like a breath of fresh air, wearing a flimsy calf-length cotton frock, the skirt pleated from the waist. This was worn without petticoats or a corset and the general effect was considered to be quite shocking, especially since she leapt about the court, which she did with all the grace of a ballerina. She had no qualms about revealing large expanses of stocking and even thigh! To complete her outfit she wore a soft linen hat.

Although there were those who thought Suzanne was wickedly daring and even indecent, she was able to get away with revolutionising all future ladies' tennis fashion in this way, because she was a wonderful player and a real star. She reigned supreme for seven years. By 1920 Suzanne was starting to perfect her new look. She returned to Wimbledon with her hair fashionably "bobbed" and sporting a "bandeau". This consisted of several yards of brightly coloured silk chiffon, swathed around the head and fastened with a strategically placed pin. Very soon, the "Lenglen Bandeau" became all the rage for fashion conscious ladies, both on and off the court, similarly, the Lenglen one-piece "frock" was almost universally adopted for everyday wear. Suzanne took its development further when she induced the top Paris couturiers to design for her, and thus introduced the first silk dresses to tennis. Over these she wore hip-length cardigans in colours to match her bandeau and she frequently wore white silk stockings, rolled to the knee. In winter she even wore a fur coat to and from the court for warmth.

Suzanne was greatly influenced by the Diaghilev Russian Ballet, based at Monte Carlo near her home in Nice. This was reflected in both her energetic but graceful style of play and in her insistence upon wearing only the softest and lightest of fabrics, almost transparent at times, permitting complete freedom of movement.

As was the case in the 19th century the fashion magazines of the day were quick to advise on styles and patterns for the new look. Lady players had dresses made up for them by seamstresses in cotton and in silk. When trunks were packed for visits to the Continent or to places as far afield as India, two or three of the "Lenglen" style tennis dresses were included as a necessary part of a lady's wardrobe and at last ladies had a lawn tennis costume in which they could move!

After Suzanne disappeared from the Wimbledon scene in 1926, Helen Wills from the U.S.A. was to dominate ladies' tennis on Centre Court until 1938. As with Lottie Dod, she recalls that when she first started to play tennis, she found it quite natural to wear her school uniform. This consisted of a white short-sleeved blouse and tie, worn over the top of a wide-pleated, calf length skirt. Accessories included a black tie, white stockings and white eyeshade, worn initially as protection against the glare of the bright Californian sunshine.

Style of dress

During the span of fourteen years that Helen Wills (Mrs. Moody) played at Wimbledon and won eight singles titles, her costume varied only slightly. She discarded the tie, altered the shape of the blouse collar and modified the length of her skirt. She also favoured a cerise-coloured lambswool cardigan. Soon the "Wills eyeshade" was being worn in place of the "Lenglen Bandeau" as lady players adopted the Wills style of dress throughout the 1930s. As with the bandeau, the Wills eyeshade became fashionable both on and off the court.

In 1929, Billie Tapscott from South Africa was the first lady with the courage to play at Wimbledon, admittedly on a back court, without stockings. It was, however, not until 1931 that Joan Lycett risked appearing on Centre Court with bare legs and ankle socks.

Helen Jacobs (left) chatting with Fred Perry. She wears the "Bermuda" length, tailored shorts she pioneered at Wimbledon, in 1933. Helen Wills (right) wears the two-piece costume and eye shade she made so fashionable throughout the 1930s.

Once stockings had been rejected, this cleared the way for shortening hemlines still further, which in turn inevitably led to the arrival of divided skirts, culottes and shorts. Interestingly, back in 1927, one lady player at Wimbledon, the attractive Lili de Alvarez from Spain, had already appeared wearing a most unusual outfit. Made for her by the Paris Couturiers, this costume took the form of a two-tiered pagoda-style tunic top, underneath which were worn flared trousers to the knee. Although considered outlandish at the time, this outfit can now be seen as being the unwitting forerunner of the divided skirts and culottes which were to become so popular from the late thirties right through the forties.

In 1933, Helen Jacobs from California pioneered the first man-tailored shorts at Wimbledon. These were "Bermuda" length with a wide navy blue stripe down both sides and worn with a short-sleeved open-necked shirt made in fine knitted wool. By the mid-thirties, culottes and divided skirts were popular, worn at lengths around two to three inches above the knee, with short-sleeved open-necked shirts and sometimes with accompanying coloured short-sleeved cardigans.

In the late thirties Alice Marble from San Francisco introduced the more aggressive "serve and volley" style of play to ladies' tennis. Appropriately, when she played, she wore clothes in keeping with her style of play. These consisted of a crew-neck cotton Tee-shirt, a jaunty jockey-cap, and shorts which were the shortest seen yet, being about six inches above the knee.

By 1939 many of the male players had given up long trousers in favour of shorts. During the 1930s "Oxford Bag" style trousers in cream wool or flannel had been very popular. These baggy trousers were worn long and voluminous, with turn-ups, and short-sleeved open-necked shirts. Cricket style sweaters were used for extra warmth, often being worn to and from the court, slung casually across the shoulders.

When in 1933 Bunny Austin wore the first men's shorts on the Centre Court at Wimbledon, his attire had been considered just as outrageous a departure from the norm as some of the innovations in ladies' costume over the years, even though by modern standards they really were extremely long shorts!

Bunny Austin was the first man to appear on Centre Court wearing shorts. The change from trousers to shorts is the single most dramatic change to occur to date, in the development of men's tennis wear.

Fred Perry and Frank Shields sporting the "Oxford Bag" style trousers and open-neck shirts popular throughout the 1930s.

When play ceased at Wimbledon because of the Second World War, the beginnings of the "unisex" look were already in evidence and all-white remained firmly entrenched as the requirement for playing attire. When Wimbledon re-opened in 1946, the Ladies' Championship was dominated, right through to the 1950s, by a line of formidable American lady players. Their names included Pauline Betz, Margaret Osborne, Louise Brough, Doris Hart, Maureen Connolly, Shirley Fry and Althea Gibson. Just after the War tennis clothing was difficult to obtain, even in the U.S.A., and therefore in the late forties and early fifties the predominating styles might be described as somewhat functional and straightforward. Quite often clothes had to be made up at home. Abbreviated, pleated white culottes were the norm, worn with matching baggy blouse-tops, which might feature split shoulder-cap sleeves. Sometimes coloured belts were added to this rather utilitarian picture.

Ted Tinling, a couturier who had by this time been involved in Tennis for more than thirty years, initially as an umpire and player on the French Riviera at the time of Suzanne Lenglen, and then from 1927 as official liaison between The Championships Committee at Wimbledon and the players, decided to attempt to make ladies' post-war tennis clothes more feminine and decorative. This resulted in Tinling creating dresses with pastel-coloured hemlines for Joy Gannon in 1947 and a dress with similar coloured trimmings for Betty Hilton for her Wightman Cup matches in 1948.

Coloured clothing

The authorities, however, of both the British and American establishments, were not impressed and this resulted in "all white" clothing remaining the rule until 1972, when the U.S. Championships were the first official international event to permit coloured tennis clothing. Even so, no one could have foreseen the furore that was to occur when in 1949, Tinling, as a compromise solution to femininity in tennis wear, added a white lace trim to the tennis knickers worn by Gussy Moran beneath her pretty dress of white rayon trimmed in satin, the hemline of which reached to within a few inches above her knees. During the twenty years that followed the "Gorgeous Gussy" incident, lady players

Margaret Osborne and Louise Brough step smartly out on court in the culottes, blouse and blazer costume typical of the styles in vogue in the late 1940s.

Maria Bueno (left) in one of the feminine styles created for her by couturier Ted Tinling, 1960. Billie Jean King (right) plays in the kilted skirt and knitted shirt outfit, popular as an alternative to Tinling's more feminine styles, 1967.

were divided in their requirements for tennis clothes. There were those such as Pauline Betz, Margaret Osborne, Louise Brough, Doris Hart and Althea Gibson who preferred the tailored look, as opposed to players such as Maureen Connolly and Shirley Fry, who preferred more feminine lines and styles.

The fifties and sixties saw the advent of man-made fabrics and synthetic fibres such as nylon, orlon and polyester. Drip-dry clothes were now a reality. The first all-nylon tennis dress was worn on Centre Court in 1951 by Britain's Pat Ward and the first disposable paper tennis dress was also worn on Centre Court, in a match played before H.R.H. Princess Anne, by Silvana Lazzarino of Italy, in 1957.

Throughout the sixties, the Fred Perry-sponsored look was very popular and was favoured by champions such as Karen Susman, Margaret Court and Billie Jean King. This consisted of a short-sleeved, white knitted shirt, worn either with a kilted skirt or tailored shorts. However, there were other players who required their tennis attire to be more feminine during the fifties and sixties and these included Maria Bueno and some other South American

Evonne Goolagong (left) in the princess-line dress designed by Tinling for her matches at Wimbledon, 1972. Chris Evert (right), whose grace on court has always delighted spectators.

players, as well as Darlene Hard, Christine Truman, Ann Jones and Lesley Turner.

Tinling, though restricted to white on the outside, compromised by producing pretty dresses for these players, with full skirts reflecting the popular fashion trends of the time, with pretty pastel linings underneath, lacy petticoats or contrasting coloured knickers. In 1962, he caused another stir when he created a "shocking pink" lining for one of Maria Bueno's dresses. Maria's graceful style of play on court reminded many tennis lovers of Suzanne Lenglen, and her "star" quality and elegance were further enhanced by the beautiful feminine dresses designed for her by Ted Tinling.

In the same year a Wimbledon ruling followed stating that tennis clothing should be "predominantly white". With the exception of a cardigan, pullover or headwear, the same ruling applies today. In 1971, Evonne Goolagong won the hearts of many Wimbledon spectators when she claimed her first singles victory and also re-established the popularity of the more feminine style of tennis wear in the process. In 1972, Chris Evert's grace on court was reflected in Mondessa's tennis wear designs which featured coloured geometric or flowered motifs and which had a graceful swing to the skirt that had been lacking in the skirts and kilts of the sixties.

The advent of the Virginia Slims Women's Pro' circuit in 1971 and of colour television led to the creation of some startling garments on the tennis court, utilising materials such as sequins, lamé and velvet. With many matches on this circuit taking place at night under spotlights in enormous stadiums in front of huge crowds, colour and glitter quickly became part of the show, enabling leading players to be identified at some distance.

Mint green

When Billie Jean King beat Bobby Riggs in an exhibition match in the vast Houston Astrodome in 1973, in front of over 30,000 spectators, she wore a dress in mint green with a royal blue insert across the front, matching her royal blue tennis shoes. Her dress was also embroidered with rhinestones and sequins in a "VS" design.

In the 1980s, Ted Tinling's feminine dresses were replaced by the co-ordinated and sponsored look, with matching shirts and skirts being made in the most appropriate of modern materials. The demise of the dress coincided with the general fashion trend of the time which was away from dresses towards skirts and tops which could be mixed and matched.

In 1985 Anne White stirred up memories of Gussy Moran when she played at Wimbledon in her controversial white figure-hugging body suit. In 1991 Centre Court spectators waited with bated breath as André Agassi, known for his flamboyantly colourful style of dress, took off his track suit for the first time, to reveal a stunning all-white outfit complete with cycling shorts worn under his tennis shorts, a shirt, which revealed more midriff than had been seen before during a serve, and a jaunty baseball cap, all much to the delight of his adoring fans. In so doing he immediately created a niche for himself in the catalogue of developments and milestones in the history of tennis costume.

The manufacture of tennis wear has become big business, with players receiving huge sums in sponsorship deals when they allow their names to be used in association with various products. As *Racquet magazine* aptly commented in 1997: "The female athlete

Steffi Graf plays in the co-ordinated shirt and skirt look of the early 1990s. André Agassi in the all-white cycling shorts and baseball hat that he wore with flair at Wimbledon in 1992.

has arrived! Today women command colossal endorsement fees, have their names emblazoned on footwear and prove their mettle with an intensity unthinkable only a few years ago. Sport for women has reached flashpoint".

Although many women players still favour the co-ordinated look, the tennis dress has recently made something of a comeback. But this time round it comes without the frills and furbelows that became its hallmark in the fifties and sixties. The look, by contrast, is sleek with smooth lines which incorporate style and femininity, without compromising movement and choice.

New materials such as cotton with lycra are both comfortable and more lightweight, whilst other fabrics actually absorb moisture and prevent clothes becoming heavy with sweat during a match. New design details incorporate collarless zip fronts, button downs with belts, pleated skirts with side slits, body suits and even cycling shorts worn beneath dresses and skirts made from lightweight materials.

Venus Williams in the lightweight halter-neck dress and shorts outfit which she wore for all her Singles matches in 2001

As the fashion world engages in the never-ending search for something completely different to wear on court, we can only guess at what eye-catching item the fashion designers will come up with next. And just what would Maud Watson or Lottie Dod have thought of it all today? Of that we can never be certain, but I am sure that they would be pleased to think that their pioneering efforts had not been in vain and that at least women were now able to enjoy the game of tennis as much as men, unhampered by petticoats, stays and the tyranny of corsets!